THE WALLFLOWER

YAMATONADESHIKO SHICHIHENGE

11

Tomoko Hayakawa

Translated and adapted by
David Ury

Lettered by
North Market Street Graphics

Ballantine Books • New York

A Del Rey Trade Paperback Original

The Wallflower copyright © 2004 by Tomoko Hayakawa.
English translation copyright © 2007 by Tomoko Hayakawa.

Published in the United States by Del Rey Books, an imprint of The Random House Publishing Group, a division of Random House, Inc., New York.

DEL REY is a registered trademark and the Del Rey colophon is a trademark of Random House, Inc.

Publication rights arranged through Kodansha Ltd.

First published in Japan in 2004 by Kodansha Ltd., Tokyo, as Yamatonadeshiko Schicihenge.

ISBN 978-0-345-49475-7

Printed in the United States of America

www.delreymanga.com

9 8 7 6 5 4 3

Translator/Adaptor—David Ury
Lettering—North Market Street Graphics

Contents

A Note from the Author

I went to Disneyland for the first time in ten years. I went because they had temporarily turned the Haunted Mansion into a *Nightmare Before Christmas*—themed ride. I was so excited (too excited). Jack looked really cute. ♥ ♥ I'm gonna go as many times as I can while the *Nightmare* stuff is still up. ♥ I wish they'd just keep the *Nightmare* theme forever instead of just having it for a limited time. I love it!

—**Tomoko Hayakawa**

Honorifics

Throughout the Del Rey Manga books, you will find Japanese honorifics left intact in the translations. For those not familiar with how the Japanese use honorifics and, more important, how they differ from American honorifics, we present this brief overview.

Politeness has always been a critical facet of Japanese culture. Ever since the feudal era, when Japan was a highly stratified society, use of honorifics—which can be defined as polite speech that indicates relationship or status—has played an essential role in the Japanese language. When addressing someone in Japanese, an honorific usually takes the form of a suffix attached to one's name (example: "Asuna-san"), or as a title at the end of one's name, or appears in place of the name itself (example: "Negi-sensei," or simply "Sensei!").

Honorifics can be expressions of respect or endearment. In the context of manga and anime, honorifics give insight into the nature of the relationship between characters. Many English translations leave out these important honorifics, and therefore distort the feel of the original Japanese. Because Japanese honorifics contain nuances that English honorifics lack, it is our policy at Del Rey not to translate them. Here, instead, is a guide to some of the honorifics you may encounter in Del Rey Manga.

-*san:* This is the most common honorific, and is equivalent to Mr., Miss, Ms., Mrs. It is the all-purpose honorific and can be used in any situation where politeness is required.

-*sama:* This is one level higher than "-san." It is used to confer great respect.

-*dono:* This comes from the word "tono," which means "lord." It is an even higher level than "-sama" and confers utmost respect.

-kun: This suffix is used at the end of boys' names to express familiarity or endearment. It is also sometimes used by men amongst friends, or when addressing someone younger or of a lower station.

-chan: This is used to express endearment, mostly toward girls. It is also used for little boys, pets, and even among lovers. It gives a sense of childish cuteness.

Bozu: This is an informal way to refer to a boy, similar to the English terms "kid" or "squirt."

Sempai/Senpai:
This title suggests that the addressee is one's senior in a group or organization. It is most often used in a school setting, where underclassmen refer to their upperclassmen as "sempai." It can also be used in the workplace, such as when a newer employee addresses an employee who has seniority in the company.

Kohai: This is the opposite of "sempai" and is used toward underclassmen in school or newcomers in the workplace. It connotes that the addressee is of a lower station.

Sensei: Literally meaning "one who has come before," this title is used for teachers, doctors, or masters of any profession or art.

[blank]: This is usually forgotten in these lists, but it is perhaps the most significant difference between Japanese and English. The lack of honorific means that the speaker has permission to address the person in a very intimate way. Usually, only family, spouses, or very close friends have this kind of permission. Known as *yobisute,* it can be gratifying when someone who has earned the intimacy starts to call one by one's name without an honorific. But when that intimacy hasn't been earned, it can be very insulting.

CONTENTS

I'M MACHAPII.

MY FANTASY IS...

HOW LOVELY!

HIS SLENDER BACK!

THE OCEAN!

KYAA KYAA KYAA

YOU'RE MORE BEAUTIFUL THAN ANY ROSE.

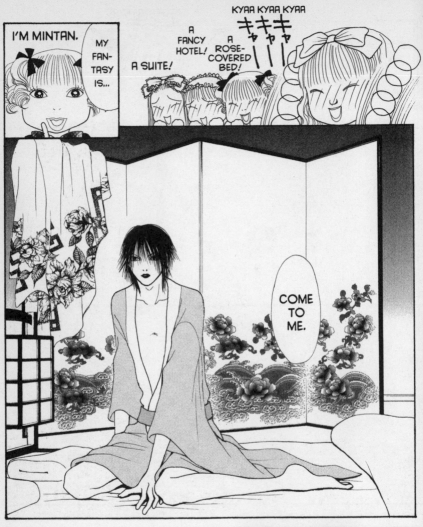

I'M MINTAN. MY FANTASY IS...

A SUITE!

A FANCY HOTEL!

A ROSE-COVERED BED!

KYAA KYAA KYAA
キャキャキャ

COME TO ME.

くるくるくるくる
SPIN   SPIN

OH MY...

DON'T BE AFRAID.

WALLFLOWER'S BEAUTIFUL CAST OF CHARACTERS (?)

SUNAKO IS A DARK LONER WHO LOVES HORROR MOVIES. WHEN HER AUNT, THE LANDLADY OF A BOARDINGHOUSE, LEAVES TOWN WITH HER BOYFRIEND, SUNAKO IS FORCED TO LIVE WITH FOUR HANDSOME GUYS. SUNAKO'S AUNT MAKES A DEAL WITH THE BOYS, WHICH CAUSES NOTHING BUT HEADACHES FOR SUNAKO. "MAKE SUNAKO INTO A LADY, AND YOU CAN LIVE RENT FREE." AND NOW WITH TAKENAGA'S TRUE LOVE, NOI-CHAN, THE GORGEOUS BISHOJO...AND THAT BEAUTIFUL PRINCESS WHO IS FALLING FOR RANMARU, IT LOOKS LIKE SUNAKO'S WORLD IS GETTING EVEN MORE BLINDINGLY BRIGHT.

KYOHEI TAKANO—A STRONG FIGHTER. "I'M THE KING."

TAKENAGA ODA—A CARING FEMINIST.

RANMARU MORII—A TRUE LADY'S MAN.

YUKINOJO TOYAMA—A GENTLE, CHEERFUL AND VERY EMOTIONAL GUY.

SUNAKO NAKAHARA

CHAPTER 43 –
BRAVO GIRLS!

PIMPLES

OILY
SKIN

BEHIND THE SCENES

PLEASE JUST READ THEM AND THINK "ALL THAT SUFFERING AND THIS IS ALL THAT CAME OF IT?" I REMEMBER HAVING SUCH A HARD TIME WITH THIS STORY THAT I BURST INTO TEARS.

THE STUFF IN THIS BOOK IS ACTUALLY FROM QUITE A WHILE AGO, BUT APPARENTLY, THAT'S THE WAY THE PUBLISHER WANTED IT.
(I REALLY DON'T UNDERSTAND WHY, BUT...)
RIGHT NOW I'M DOING A BIT BETTER, BUT BACK WHEN I WROTE THESE STORIES, I WAS HAVING A REALLY, REALLY HARD TIME. THE "BEHIND THE SCENES" SECTIONS ARE ALL REALLY NEGATIVE. DON'T PAY TOO MUCH ATTENTION TO THEM.

TAPPA
TAPPA

バババ
バ
バ
バ……

UH,
UM...

E-
EXCUSE
ME.

I MEAN,
NOI-CHAN
DOES IT ALL
THE TIME, BUT...

Y-YOU'RE
JUST
GONNA
LET THEM
RUN
AWAY?

バ
バ
バ
バ
バ
TAPPA
TAPPA
……

TH-THEY

LOOK

RIGHT,
TAKENAGA?

BUT SHE
CAME
OVER HERE
JUST TO
SEE YOU,
RANMARU.

IT'S
NOT LIKE
WE'RE
GOING
OUT OR
ANYTHING.

IT'S
NO
BIG
DEAL.

PERFECT

TOGETHER...

GO
ASK
HER.

HOW
THE
HELL
SHOULD
I
KNOW?

AND I KNOW HE HAS A LOT OF GIRLS AFTER HIM.

HE'S NOT EVEN INTERESTED IN ME.

YOU'D BETTER TURN HIM DOWN NOW WHILE YOU STILL CAN.

YOU KNOW, IF YOU MARRY RANMARU, YOU'RE GONNA HAVE AN AWFULLY ROUGH LIFE.

BUT HE'S SO SWEET. I THINK HE'S JUST WAITING FOR ME TO CALL IT OFF...

SO I'VE BEEN TAKING ADVANTAGE OF HIS KINDNESS AND PUTTING OFF MY ANSWER FOR AS LONG AS POSSIBLE.

M-MARRY HIM?

I JUST DON'T WANT IT TO END.

DRIP DRIP

NEVER SAY NEVER!

B-BUT I COULD NEVER...

I ONCE READ THAT... CONFIDENCE IS THE KEY TO A WOMAN'S BEAUTY.

...MAKE RANMARU-KUN FALL HEAD OVER HEELS FOR YOU.

WHAT YOU NEED TO DO IS GET RID OF THE COMPETITION, AND..

YOU'RE THE ONLY ONE WHO COULD TRULY LOVE THAT FOOL.

I'M PRETTY SURE...

WELCOME.

COOL! I'VE ALWAYS WANTED TO COME TO A PLACE LIKE THIS. ♥

WH-WHAT HAPPENED TO ITALY?

AH, SHE'S WITH US.

WAH.

...AND CHANGE INTO THESE PANTS. ♥

PLEASE UNDRESS...

RIGHT THIS WAY.

HELP ME!

たーすけて

SURE, SHE COULD USE A ROUGH MASSAGE.

AHH, THAT FEELS GOOD.

DO YOU THINK SUNAKO-SAN IS OKAY?

BUT SHE JUST DOESN'T HAVE ANY SELF-CONFIDENCE.

SUNAKO-CHAN IS ACTUALLY REALLY BEAUTIFUL. SHE'S SO COOL.

BUT YOU SEEM SO FULL OF CONFIDENCE.

TRUST ME, I'M NOT.

I'D LIKE TO BE MORE CONFIDENT.

ME, TOO.

I NEED TO WORK ON MY OWN CONFIDENCE.

I'M SURE SOME DAY SHE'LL REALIZE JUST HOW BEAUTIFUL SHE REALLY IS.

キャッ キャッ KYAA KYAA

YOUR SKIN IS SO SMOOTH AND SOFT. I'M SO JEALOUS.

YOUR SKIN IS MUCH NICER THAN MINE, NOI-SAN.

ぺか

SPARKLE

-24-

ひぃぃぃっ
KYAAA

ひぃぃぃっ
KYAAA

WHY DON'T YOU JUST COME TO MY HOUSE?

LET'S BUY SOME MAKEUP BEFORE WE HEAD HOME.

NOW...

THINK OF THIS AS *A TEST.*

THE POOR THING...

SUNAKO -CHAN.

PAT PAT
ぽむぽむ

OKAY. I PROMISE I WON'T GO INTO SHOCK NO MATTER HOW HUGE IT IS.

ばたり
THUD

KYAA!

-29-

THWINK

YES, IT'S DELICIOUS.

ISN'T IT?

ISN'T IT?

ISN'T IT GOOD?

THANK YOU, SUNAKO-CHAN. IT'S SO GOOD!

YUM. ♥

AH.

DRIP

DROP

DRIP

DRIP

DRIP

DRIP

DRIP

...I JUST CAN'T HOLD BACK MY TEARS.

I'M SORRY. I'M TRYING TO HAVE A NICE TIME, BUT...

I-I'M SURE HE DIDN'T MEAN THAT. HE WAS JUST TRYING TO GET BACK AT KYOHEI.

NO, HE WASN'T.

SNIFF

I GUESS I WAS WRONG.

I THOUGHT THAT TAKENAGA-KUN AND I WERE A COUPLE...

I-I...

SNEAK

NOI-CHAN...

SORRY.

I DIDN'T MEAN IT.

-44-

GRUMBLE

GRUMBLE

MAYBE I WAS A LITTLE TOO HARD ON THEM.

PLUP

SIGH

YAY!

OKAY, YOU CAN ALL COME AND EAT NOW...

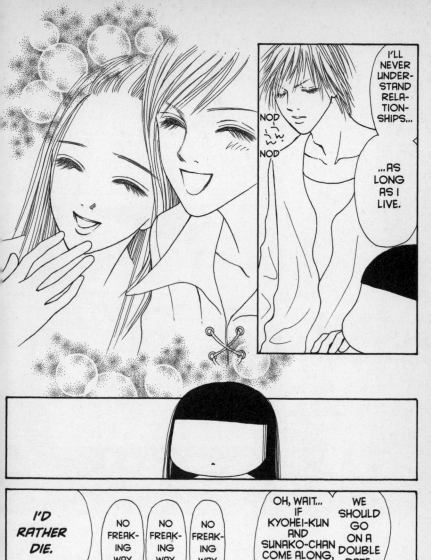

I'LL NEVER UNDERSTAND RELATIONSHIPS...

...AS LONG AS I LIVE.

NOD NOD

I'D RATHER DIE.

NO FREAKING WAY.

NO FREAKING WAY.

NO FREAKING WAY.

THAT SOUNDS LIKE FUN.

OH, WAIT... IF KYOHEI-KUN AND SUNAKO-CHAN COME ALONG, WE COULD MAKE IT A TRIPLE DATE. ♥

WE SHOULD GO ON A DOUBLE DATE.

KYA KYA

CHAPTER 44 –

THE TEST OF LOVE

PLEASE STAY OUT OF MY ROOM.

I'LL HAVE DINNER READY IN A SECOND, SO...

SMASH

WOBBLE

RIGHT, HIROSHI?

THESE ARE JUST DOLLS. THEY CAN'T TALK.

OOPS, SORRY.

PAT PAT

YOU ARE SO FREAKING SCARY.

BEHIND THE SCENES

I HAD A MONTH OFF ♥ BETWEEN THE LAST STORY AND THIS ONE. BUT, SINCE I ALWAYS BARELY MAKE MY DEADLINES, I DECIDED TO SPEND THAT MONTH WORKING ON THE STORY. I SPENT MY WHOLE VACATION WORKING. BUT MY EDITOR STILL DIDN'T GIVE MY STORYBOARDS THE OKAY. *A WEEK BEFORE MY DEADLINE, I HAD TO START OVER FROM SCRATCH...* I WAS SERIOUSLY CONSIDERING JUST RUNNING AWAY. (I HAD MY BAGS PACKED.) I GOT FED UP WITH MY OWN LACK OF TALENT. I KNOW I'M NOT THAT TALENTED, BUT DID THEY REALLY HAVE TO RUB IT IN?

KYAAAA

IT'S JUST A DOLL, DAMN IT! IS A DOLL MORE IMPORTANT THAN A REAL LIVE PERSON?

WELL, WHAT DO YOU EXPECT? YOU KNOCKED OVER HER "BEST FRIEND."

I CAN'T BELIEVE SHE SCRATCH-ED ME.

IT REALLY STUNG IN THE BATH.

IT IS TO SUNAKO-CHAN.

WHA-WHAA?

AND ONE MORE TIME, YEAH!

YEAH!

YEAH!

I WAS A HUGE CHO-SAN FAN.

SO YOU DO GET IT.

HIROSHI-KUN IS A *DOLL,* SO HE CAN'T EAT ANYWAY.

BLUSH

...HATES GREEN TEA ICE CREAM.

HIROSHI...

AND YET YOU STILL CARE MORE ABOUT YOUR DOLLS THAN YOU DO ABOUT REAL PEOPLE.

WELL, MORE THAN I DO ABOUT YOU ANYWAY

SHOCK

THAT WAS HOGEN DOZZ GREEN TEA ICE CREAM...

GRR

KYOHEI!

I FOUND HIM IN THE GARBAGE BEHIND THE ELEMENTARY SCHOOL.

I LOVE JOSEPHINE AND AKIRA-KUN, TOO, BUT...

HIROSHI-KUN IS SPECIAL.

HEY, HIROSHI-KUN...

YOU'RE SO SPECIAL, HIROSHI-KUN.

SQUEEZE

HIS GUTS? WE THREW THOSE OUT A LONG TIME AGO.

IT SCARES THE KIDS.

WE DON'T NEED IT, SO GO AHEAD AND TAKE IT.

...CREATURE OF THE LIGHT EVER COULD.

SQUEEZE SQUEEZE

HE UNDERSTANDS ME MUCH BETTER THAN ANY...

SQUEEZE

YOU'RE THE ONLY ONE WHO UNDERSTANDS ME.

NOBODY EVER TAKES MY SIDE.

DON'T YOU?

DON'T YOU FEEL BAD FOR ME?

RUSTLE

...HOW SUNAKO NAKAHARA FEELS.

I'M STARTING TO UNDERSTAND...

I CAME HERE JUST HOPING TO CATCH A GLIMPSE OF KYOHEI-KUN, BUT...

I CAN'T BELIEVE WHAT WE JUST SAW.

YEAH.

D-DID YOU SEE THAT?

...CREEPY DOLL. ♥

KYOHEI-KUN REALLY LOVES THIS...

TH-THE HACHIOUJI POLICE DEPARTMENT?

HELLO?

YEAH, BUT I DON'T THINK SHE EVEN TOOK HER PURSE.

IF HIROSHI-KUN IS AT STAKE, THERE'S NO TELLING WHAT SHE MIGHT DO.

DON'T BLAME THE MESSENGER!

SHE MADE IT THAT FAR?

RING RING RING

WE'VE GOT SCHOOL TOMORROW, SO I'M SURE SHE'LL COME BACK HOME.

SHE'LL BE FINE. IT'S NOT LIKE SHE'S A LITTLE KID OR SOMETHING.

SHE WAS FOUND LYING OUTSIDE UNCONSCIOUS.

SHE MUST HAVE...

...WALKED FOR HOURS WITHOUT EATING OR DRINKING ANYTHING.

SNIFFLE
SNIFF

I GUESS...

THERE'S NOT MUCH WE CAN DO.

IT'S JUST A FREAKING DOLL.

THIS IS SO STUPID.

WOULD YOU QUIT SAYING THAT?

SHE'S PROBABLY SOME-WHERE IN HERE.

HER SHOES ARE HERE, AND ALL THE DOORS IN THE HOUSE ARE OPEN, SO...

IT'S FIVE AM...

WAKE UP. WAKE UP.

SUNAKO-CHAN IS GONE!

KYOHEI!

YOU TAKE NORTH, KYOHEI.

YAWN

SCRATCH SCRATCH
ボリ ボリ

WE'LL SPLIT INTO NORTH, SOUTH, EAST, AND WEST!

バタ バタ
TAPPA TAPPA

TAPPA

LET'S SPLIT UP AND LOOK FOR HER!

か゛チャ
CLICK

GOD...

—65—

YOU
NEED
TO
CALM
DOWN.

YEAH, JUST GET SOME REST.

SUNAKO-CHAN...

YOU DON'T HAVE TO GO TO SCHOOL TODAY.

NO, I'LL GO...

THE TOAST IS BURNING.

TAPPA TAPPA

SMELLS LIKE SOMETHING'S BURNING.

THE EGGS ARE BURNT, TOO.

SLICE

WAAAAHH うわああ—— んっっっ

WE'RE SORRY. WE'RE SORRY.

SHE'S SO SCARY. SHE'S SO SCARY.

I GUESS HE'S NOT IN THERE.

SIGH ふぅしゅう HISSS

I'VE GOT AN IDEA.

WAIT...

LET'S JUST THROW IT AWAY, AND NEVER TELL A SOUL.

THAT COULD'VE BEEN US.

I-I GUESS IT WAS NAKAHARA-SAN'S.

WE'D BETTER GIVE IT BACK.

くるくるくる
SPIN SPIN

STEP
スタッ

BUT THERE IS A CATCH.

MOVED
きゅうん

AWW, SHE LOOKS SO CUTE. ♥

L-LET'S GO! RIGHT NOW!

IT'S A GOOD DEAL FOR EVERY-BODY.

YOU'LL GET YOUR DOLL BACK, AND...

KYAA, SHE SAID IT. ♥♥♥♥

WE'LL GET TO HAVE KYOHEI-KUN OVER. ♥

SHE LIVES ALL BY HERSELF.

WE WANT KYOHEI-KUN TO COME OVER AND PICK IT UP. ♥

HAPPY?

I'M FREEZING.

ARE YOU OKAY, KYOHEI?

I KNEW IT.

YEAH, SHE'D NEVER HUG KYOHEI.

ME, TOO.

THEN THEY TORE OFF MY SCHOOL JACKET AND MY SHIRT. I GUESS THAT WAS ENOUGH TO SATISFY THEM.

FIRST I HAD TEA AND CAKE WITH THEM.

THEY WEREN'T SATISFIED. THEY JUST PASSED OUT.

GUSHING NOSEBLEEDS

THANKS.

TONIGHT'S DINNER BETTER BE GOOD.

OKAY!

P-PLEASE DON'T HIT ME.

I'LL BRING MORE TOMORROW.

I...

THIS IS ALL YOU HAVE?

FWICK

IT'S JUST YOUR TYPICAL, AVERAGE TOKYO PUBLIC SCHOOL.

THIS IS MORI HIGH SCHOOL.

TSSSS

MORE OR LESS.

SAYING THAT JUST MAKES ME WANNA HIT YOU EVEN HARDER—

DRIP DRIP

ROLL ROLL

FLASH

CHAPTER 45 –
SUNAKO THE CHAMPION

FLASH

A-A
GHOST!

KYAAAA!

THE ONE
PECULIAR
THING
ABOUT
MORI
HIGH
SCHOOL
IS...

...THAT
NUMEROUS
STRANGE
PHENOMENON
HAVE BEEN
WITNESSED
ON ITS
CAMPUS.

SIGH. I SHOULD'VE BROUGHT MY UMBRELLA.

WH-WHAT WAS THAT...

I FEEL A WEIRD PRESENCE IN HERE.

SHE HAD ABSOLUTELY NO IDEA.

NEARLY ALL OF THEM WERE CAUSED BY HER, BUT...

BEHIND THE SCENES

I DON'T EVEN WANNA REMEMBER THIS. SERIOUSLY. AFTER WHAT HAPPENED LAST TIME, I WAS REALLY SCARED ABOUT MAKING MY DEADLINES. I WORKED EVERY SINGLE DAY WITHOUT A BREAK. I TURNED DOWN EVERY INVITATION FROM FRIENDS WHO WANTED TO GO OUT. KIYOHARU HAD A CONCERT JUST BEFORE MY DEADLINE. ♥ BUT I JUST COULDN'T FINISH ON TIME. I CRIED EVERY DAY. I CRIED LIKE CRAZY WHEN I MET MY EDITOR. THAT HAD NEVER HAPPENED TO ME BEFORE.

I ENDED UP NOT GOING TO THE KIYOHARU CONCERT...

I CRIED AS I WORKED EVEN THOUGH MY ASSISTANT WAS RIGHT NEXT TO ME.

LOVE CHANGES A WOMAN.

I'VE GOT TO SHOW HIM HOW PRETTY I CAN BE. I'VE GOT TO SHOW HIM HOW BEAUTIFUL I CAN BE.

AND BEFORE YOU KNOW IT...

FWISH

SHE'S A LADY!

WHAT?

SIGH

I WISH SUNAKO NAKAHARA WOULD JUST FIND A *BOYFRIEND* ALREADY.

THEY'RE *PERFECT* FOR EACH OTHER

WELL, NEITHER DOES SUNAKO-CHAN.

KYOHEI JUST DOESN'T GET IT...

FLASH

NOT THIS LADY CRAP AGAIN...

I'M HAPPY THE WAY I AM.

THE ONLY THING THE SUN IS GOOD FOR IS DRYING CLOTHES.

TCH. DAMN IT, IT WAS SUCH A NICE DAY YESTER-DAY.

I DON'T WANNA CHANGE.

SHADE.

FWOOSH

SHADE.

AH

YOU'D BETTER GET OUT OF HERE!

LET'S GO!

AAAHHHH

TA-TAKANO!

SNAP OUT OF IT.

I WAS ON MY WAY TO THE LIBRARY.

SLAP

AH

IF THEY FIND OUT, WE'RE GONNA HAVE TO *PAY* FOR 'EM, YOU KNOW?

YOU SHATTERED ALL THE LIGHT-BULBS AGAIN, DIDN'T YOU?

HE'S JUST LIKE ME. ♥

ULTRA RARE

I FOUND THIS IN THEIR WAREHOUSE.

HISTORY OF THE DEAD

MY PARENTS RUN A *BOOKSTORE.*

LET'S BE FRIENDS.

WITH YOU AS A FRIEND, I THINK I CAN REALLY CHANGE.

THANK YOU. THANK YOU.

DARK MEETS DARKER...

WELL, MISERY LOVES COMPANY.

SOME PEOPLE ARE CREATURES OF THE LIGHT...

...AND SOME PREFER TO LIVE IN DARKNESS.

STOP TRYING TO FORCE YOUR BELIEFS ON US.

ぎゃんぎゃん
KYAA   KYAA

IDIOTS.

SO...

THERE IS NO TRICK.

TEACH ME THE TRICK TO GOING *DEEPER INTO THE DARKNESS.*

WHAT EXACTLY DO YOU WANT ME TO DO?

UM...

UH...

まあステキ♡
KYAA. ♥

HEY.

DO YOU WANNA COME SEE MY FAMILY'S WAREHOUSE TODAY?

SWISH スカ

SWISH スカ

SWISH スカ

THAT WAS AMAZING!

I CAN'T BELIEVE YOU DID THAT!

CLAP パチパチパチ CLAP

I'LL LET YOU OFF EASY TODAY, GEEK.

TAPPA TAPPA バタバタ

CALM けろりっ

ぜぜぜ

PANT PANT っっっ

CLAP CLAP パチパチ

WELL, WANNA PRACTICE?

OF COURSE YOU'LL JUST BE FIGHTING AGAINST ME.

I DON'T EVEN KNOW HOW TO DEFEND MYSELF.

WOW, I'M SO JEALOUS.

"MISERY LOVES COMPANY."

"I DON'T THINK I'D STAND A CHANCE."

THEY WERE WAITING FOR ME YESTERDAY.

IF ONLY... IF ONLY YOU'D BEEN THERE, NAKAHARA-SAN...

...THEN IT WOULD NEVER HAVE COME TO THIS.

SNIFF

SNIFF

THEY DON'T USE IT ANYMORE, SO NO ONE EVER GOES IN THERE.

DON'T YOU KNOW WHERE IT IS? IT'S THAT BUILDING BEHIND THE BIKE RACKS.

PLEASE COME WITH ME!

THE AUDITORIUM?

TH-THEY TOLD ME TO WAIT FOR THEM IN THE AUDITORIUM.

WHAT, YOU WANT ME AROUND 24/7?

N-NO... THAT'S NOT WHAT I MEANT...

THE GEEK'S LATE.

I CAN'T STAND SEEING PEOPLE DIE.

I LOVE CORPSES, BUT...

NA-NAKAHARA-SAN.

WHEN YOU SAID YOU WANTED TO CHANGE...

WHAT THE HELL DID YOU MEAN?

I TOLD YOU. YOU DON'T HAVE WHAT IT TAKES TO BE LIKE SUNAKO NAKAHARA.

THEY'RE...

NOD NOD

SUNAKO-CHAN AND KYOHEI ARE PERFECT FOR EACH OTHER.

I DON'T CARE WHAT THEY SAY.

GOOD MORNING!

WHAT THE HELL?

NOW THAT'S DEFINITELY NOT GONNA HAPPEN.

THAT'S MY NEW GOAL!

I WANNA BE JUST LIKE YOU, TAKANO-KUN!

CHAPTER 46 –
WHAT IS LOVE?

BEHIND THE SCENES

I HAVEN'T HAD ANY FUN FOR FOUR MONTHS. I'M REALLY REACHING MY LIMIT. (BUT I WON'T GET TO HAVE ANY FUN FOR A WHILE.) WHILE I WROTE THIS STORY, I WAS WORKING ON CORRECTING THE FIRST PRINTING OF VOLUME 10, AND WRITING A ONE SHOT FOR A *BEKKAN FRIEND* BONUS ISSUE. (IT'S IN THE FIRST PART OF THIS BOOK.) I WAS SO STRESSED OUT. THERE WAS NO WAY I COULD HAVE ANY FUN.

IT WAS SUCH A HARD TIME FOR ME. I'M USUALLY A REALLY POSITIVE PERSON, BUT ALL I COULD THINK ABOUT WAS QUITTING AND RUNNING AWAY. EVERY TIME I MISS A DEADLINE, I CAUSE TROUBLE FOR EVERYBODY AROUND ME. I STARTED TO REALLY HATE MYSELF WHEN I REALIZED HOW MUCH TROUBLE I WAS CAUSING. I'VE GOTTA FIGURE OUT HOW TO GET THOUGH THIS. AAAHHH.

DINNER'S ALMOST READY.

WHAT'S WRONG, RANMARU?

HE'S ALWAYS BEEN WEIRD.

TOLD YOU HE WAS ACTING WEIRD.

WHAT'S WITH HIM?

TAPPA

TAPPA

G-GET AWAY FROM ME!

KNOCK KNOCK

コンコン

RANMARU? ガチャ CLICK

NO, BUT THIS IS DIFFERENT!

HE'S REALLY FALLEN IN LOVE WITH HIMSELF THIS TIME.

HE'S ALWAYS LIKE THIS.

SEE?

SNIFFLE

SNIFF

PAT

HEY, RANMARU.

WHACK

THIS IS ALL YOUR FAULT!

SHE WOULDN'T BE RUNNING AROUND HERE LIKE SHE'S OUR LITTLE SLAVE.

RAN-MARU...

IF YOU'D ONLY TREATED SUNAKO-CHAN MORE LIKE A PERSON...

IF YOU'D ONLY MADE HER YOUR GIRL-FRIEND...

KYOHEI!

?

?

?

TAKE IT OUT ON YOU?

DON'T TAKE IT OUT ON US!

ミ!! SHOCK く。

DID YOU GET *DUMPED* BY YOUR DATE LAST NIGHT?

FWISH

IT'S ALL YOUR FREAKING FAULT! YOU'RE AFRAID TO TAKE ACTION!

DON'T WORRY, I'LL TALK SUNAKO-CHAN INTO IT.

HEY, THIS ONE SOUNDS RIGHT UP YOUR ALLEY, KYOHEI.

MAYBE HE JUST NEEDS A GOOD ASS KICKING.

HE'S REALLY STARTING TO PISS ME OFF.

ばっ
FLUP

USE THESE TO SHOW YOUR MADEMOISELLE...

...THE TRUE MEANING OF ROMANCE.

THESE ARE—

—TH—

...GOING OUTSIDE.

I'M NOT...

QUIVER
ピク

THIS IS A DEATH MATCH.

BUT...

I HAVE ABSOLUTELY NO INTEREST IN PRO WRESTLING.

BUT THESE ARE REALLY GOOD SEATS.

7°
FWIP!

DEATH MATCH...
DEATH...MATCH...
DEATH...D-E-A-T-H

BLOODBATH...
DEATH MATCH...

I MEAN, WHY DO YOU THINK THEY CALL IT A *DEATH MATCH?*

IT'S GONNA BE A REAL *BLOODBATH.*

DEATH MATCH...

AAAAHHH

THESE ARE SUCH GOOD SEATS.

OH NO, IT ALREADY STARTED.

HE TRICKED ME...

THAT BASTARD...

...AGAIN.

HE TRICKED ME...

 THUD

ほぉっと···

BLOOD...

SPLATTER

I'M GOING HOME.

SEE? NOTHING GOOD EVER COMES FROM GOING OUTSIDE

FORGET THIS!

COMPLETELY SATISFIED. ♥

FREEBIES →

ハッ AH
ハッ AH

A MOVIE! LET'S GO SEE A MOVIE!

あわわわわ
SHIVER SHIVER

W-WAIT.

WELL, I'M OUT OF HERE.

...GREATEST LOVE STORY EVER TOLD.

SCREEN 4 | 10:00~ | 12:00~ | 14:00~ | 1

GO FIGURE....

SNIFFLE SNIFF
ぐすぐす

YOU'RE SUCH A CRYBABY, MI-CHAN.

FLIP
じた じた
FLOP

I CAN'T HELP IT...

POKE

THAT'S WHAT I LOVE ABOUT YOU. ♥

SO THAT'S A "DATE"...

QUIT STARING. YOU'LL RUIN THEIR DATE.

STARE

YOU WANT ME TO DO THAT?

NO WAY, RANMARU...

CRACK   CRACK   CRACK

AAAHHHH.

WHAT THE HELL DO YOU THINK YOU'RE DOING?

YEAH, WE CAME TO SEE A HOT, STEAMY *DATE.*

WE DIDN'T COME HERE JUST TO SEE YOU TWO HANG OUT LIKE *FRIENDS.*

YOU'RE ON YOUR OWN.

HELP ME.

T-TAKENAGA! Y-YUKI!

TRY TREATING HER LIKE ONE.

SUNAKO-CHAN IS A GIRL!

SHOW SUNAKO-CHAN SOME RESPECT.

GOT IT?

じゃ CLINK

I USUALLY WAIT FOR MOVIES TO COME OUT ON DVD.

I GUESS GOING OUTSIDE DOES HAVE ITS PLUSES.

MAYBE I'LL START COMING TO THE THEATER TO GET PROGRAMS.

THAT'S OKAY.

I'M HAPPY JUST BEING WITH YOU.

SORRY, I DON'T HAVE THE MONEY TO TAKE YOU OUT ON A FANCY DATE.

SLIDE

HELLO.

AH...

SHIVER

FWISH

CHATTER CHATTER

WH-WHAT'S A HOT BISHONEN BOY LIKE HIM DOING IN THIS DUMP?

ONE *LIVER* STICK!

AHH

I'VE NEVER BEEN TO A *YAKITORI* RESTAURANT BEFORE. ♥

ONE SALTED *GIZZARD* STICK!

THUNK

AHH.

WE
HAD
FUN.
THAT'S
ALL
THAT
MATTERS.

FWAH

ぷ———ん...

WE'RE HOME.

UH.

WHAT THE—?

IT STINKS LIKE ROSES IN HERE.

WHAT'S ALL THIS?

GOOD. YOU'RE FINALLY HOME.

LEAVE HIM ALONE. KYOHEI IS FINE THE WAY HE IS...

YOU TWO ARE LUCKY. I'VE DECIDED TO DO WHATEVER IT TAKES TO CHANGE YOUR LIVES FOR THE BETTER.

CONTINUED IN WALLFLOWER BOOK 12

I'M TENNOSUKE HAYAKAWA.

HE'S SO CUTE! I LOVE HIM. ♥

HE'S LIKE A SPOILED LITTLE PRINCE.

IT'S BEEN ONE YEAR SINCE TEN CAME INTO MY LIFE.

HE USED TO FIT IN THE PALM OF MY HAND, BUT HE'S GOTTEN SO BIG.

MY DRAWINGS OF HIM ARE ALWAYS REALLY BAD, SO IT'S TIME FOR A FULL-ON PHOTO SHOOT!

HE LIES ON MY DESK WHILE I WORK.

I CAN'T DECIDE WHETHER HE'S IN MY WAY OR NOT....JUST KIDDING, HE'S DEFINITELY IN THE WAY.

HE CAN DRINK WATER FROM THE TAP ALL BY HIMSELF. ♥

SOMETIMES HE CAN'T QUITE GET AT IT.

HE'S ON TOP OF MY STORYBOARDS.

HE SLEEPS HIGH ABOVE THE WORLD.

THIS IS WHERE HE GOES AT NIGHT, OR WHEN THE WEATHER'S BAD.

HE'LL ONLY EAT FROM MY HAND.

I HOPE THESE PHOTOS COME OUT OKAY. ♥

I HAD SUCH A BUSY SCHEDULE...

IT'D BEEN NINE MONTHS SINCE I'D SEEN

THE LOVE OF MY LIFE,

THAT'S IMPOSSIBLE! NO WONDER I THOUGHT I'D DIE FROM OVERWORK!
I WAS SO NERVOUS IT REMINDED ME OF THE FIRST TIME I WENT TO A KIYOHARU CONCERT.

I WENT TO SEE...

KIYOHARU TOKYO MONTHLY ACT VOL. 1
~The first show at the 3 floors~
SHIBUYA O EAST

OH MY GOD! IT WAS SUCH AN *AWESOME* SHOW. ♥♥♥

HIS PERFORMANCE WAS VERY SUBDUED ♥ LAST TIME I SAW HIM IN CONCERT, BUT THIS TIME HE PLAYED SOME UPBEAT DANCE SONGS, TOO. HE ALSO PLAYED SOME BALLADS.

I'VE SAID IT OVER A MILLION TIMES ALREADY, BUT...
KIYOHARU IS SO GORGEOUS. ♥

I WAS REALLY HAPPY BECAUSE HE PLAYED LOTS OF KUROYUME & SADS SONGS.

I LOVE HIS NEW SONGS BUT AS A FAN, IT'S SO EXCITING TO HEAR SONGS THAT I NEVER THOUGHT I'D HEAR LIVE AGAIN. THERE'RE SOOOO MANY SONGS I LOVE.

HE EVEN DID A COVER OF A T-REX SONG. THEY'RE ONE OF MY FAVORITE BANDS. ♥ ...I COULDN'T FIGURE OUT WHICH SONG HE WAS PLAYING FOR A WHILE, BECAUSE HE PLAYED A TOTALLY DIFFERENT VERSION...

I WISH I NEVER HAD TO BLINK. I DIDN'T WANNA MISS A SECOND OF THE SHOW. I ACTUALLY DIDN'T BLINK. HE WAS SO COOL IT MADE ME CRY. (SERIOUSLY)

FOR SOME REASON, I KEPT REMINDING MYSELF, "THIS IS KIYOHARU. THIS IS THE REAL KIYOHARU." (I THINK I WAS GOING CRAZY DURING THE SHOW.)

I WENT TO SEE...

MIYAVI – AT THE BUDOKAN "THIS IS ROYAL ROAD"

I HADN'T SLEPT FOR THREE DAYS PRIOR TO THE SHOW. I WAS SO EXHAUSTED.

THAT DAY HAPPENED TO BE MY *DEADLINE!*

I'M SO SLEEPY.

I HADN'T WORN MAKEUP FOR A MONTH.

I TOOK A SHOWER FOR THE FIRST TIME IN FIVE DAYS.

IT WAS *HILARIOUS.*

HE LOOKED GREAT IN THE TRADITIONAL JAPANESE WEDDING OUTFIT. SO CUTE. ♥

MASA-KUN PLAYED THE GROOM, AND ONE OF THE EMPLOYEES FROM THE RECORD COMPANY PLAYED THE BRIDE. (IT WAS A GUY WEARING TONS OF MAKE UP)

THE PRESS-ONLY AFTER PARTY WAS SET UP LIKE A WEDDING RECEPTION THAT DAY.

HE ACTUALLY HAD GRAY HAIR THAT DAY, BUT I PERSONALLY LIKE IT THIS WAY. ♥ HE LOOKS SO GOOD WITH BLACK HAIR. ♥

I LIKE HIS SHARP EYES. ♥

PAT

MASA-KUN IS TALL! HIS HANDS ARE HUGE, TOO.

WOW, THAT'S AMAZING.

WHEN PS COMPANY PRESIDENT OZAKI-SAMA, WHO PLAYED THE GROOM'S MOTHER, TOLD MASA-KUN ABOUT WHAT I'D BEEN THROUGH, HE SAID...

HE MADE ME FEEL SO OLD.

IT STILL MADE ME *BLUSH.*

I KNEW ALL ABOUT IT, BUT...

I'D HEARD THAT MASA-KUN PATS HIS FAN'S HEADS INSTEAD OF SHAKING THEIR HANDS.

WHAT'RE YOU DOING MAKING AN OLD LADY BLUSH, YOUNGSTER?

BLUSH

HE WILL BE RELEASING A RECORD THROUGH A MAJOR LABEL AROUND THE TIME THIS BOOK COMES OUT. CONGRATULATIONS. I WISH YOU THE BEST, MASA-KUN/ MASA-KUN'S SONGS ARE AWESOME. ♥ I LOVE HIS DEEP, HUSKY VOICE. ♥ I LIKE "FUMINSHO NO NEMURIHIME (INSOMNIAC SLEEPING BEAUTY)" AND "COO QUACK CLUCK". ♥

GIFT

THE DRUMMER HIRO-KUN IS KIND OF LIKE MY FRIEND KAI-CHAN'S LITTLE BROTHER. SO I GUESS THAT MEANS HE'S MY LITTLE BROTHER, TOO (OR COULD HE BE MY SON?) HIRO-KUN IS SUCH A GOOD BOY. ♥ IF YOU SEE HIM, PLEASE GIVE HIM MY LOVE. ♥

I'VE BEEN GOING TO BOXING MATCHES LATELY. THE PROFESSIONAL BOXER OGURA IS A REALLY GREAT GUY. HE'S SO COOL WHEN HE'S FIGHTING. I'M A SATORU SUZUKI FAN. ♥

YOU MIGHT BE WONDERING WHY I'M NOT WRITING ANYTHING ABOUT BAROQUE.

THAT'S BECAUSE I DON'T WANNA THINK ABOUT THEM. IT MAKES ME SAD WHENEVER I THINK ABOUT THEM. I'VE BEEN CRYING EVER SINCE I SAW THEIR FINAL SHOW.

THANK YOU FOR BUYING KODANSHA COMICS. ♥

I DIDN'T GET TO THANK YOU GUYS EARLIER BECAUSE OF ALL THE EXTRA BONUS PAGES. SORRY ABOUT THAT.

I'M SO SORRY I WROTE SO MUCH NEGATIVE STUFF ON THE "BEHIND THE SCENES" PAGES. NOW I HAVE TIME TO GO OUT, SO I'M FEELING MUCH BETTER. I'M DOING OKAY.

I THOUGHT I'D GO CRAZY WHEN I WAS WORKING EVERY DAY WITHOUT A BREAK, BUT YOUR LETTERS KEPT ME GOING. THANK YOU SOOOOOO MUCH. I CAN NEVER THANK YOU ALL ENOUGH.

THERE ARE PEOPLE WHO TELL ME, "YOUR MANGA REALLY CHEERS ME UP." YOU GUYS ARE THE ONES WHO CHEER ME UP. (YOU GUYS ARE SO SWEET.)

I APOLOGIZE TO THOSE OF YOU WHO KEEP SAYING, "I HAVE NO IDEA WHO YOU'RE TALKING ABOUT IN YOUR BONUS PAGES." I OFTEN USE THE BONUS PAGES TO SHOW MY APPRECIATION TOWARDS PEOPLE WHO'VE TAKEN CARE OF ME (VERY WELL). OH, YEAH, AND I GUESS I WRITE ABOUT MY FRIENDS A LOT, TOO. I DIDN'T WRITE TOO MUCH ABOUT MY FRIENDS THIS TIME.

THANKS FOR DEALING WITH MY DEEP LOVE FOR TEN. BLUSH. I JUST CAN'T HELP IT. I LOVE TEN SO MUCH. THANKS FOR SENDING ME PHOTOS OF YOUR PETS. ♥ IT'S SO NICE TO SEE THEM. ♥

THANK YOU TO ALL OF YOU WHO SENT ME PRESENTS. I TREASURE THEM. ♥

I KNOW I'VE SAID THIS BEFORE, BUT REALLY, I'M GRATEFUL JUST TO RECEIVE LETTERS FROM YOU. PLEASE STOP SAYING, "SORRY FOR SENDING YOU A LETTER WITHOUT A GIFT." I'M SO HAPPY TO RECEIVE YOUR LETTERS!

HERE'S WHAT'S GOING ON IN MY LIFE NOW. I'M ON A SERIOUS DIET. MY WHOLE BODY IS SWOLLEN, AND IT LOOKS PRETTY BAD. IT'S SO HARD TO LOSE WEIGHT... I HOPE I HAVE A SUCCESS STORY FOR YOU IN BOOK 12! IF ANYBODY KNOWS A *SIMPLE* WAY TO LOSE WEIGHT, PLEASE LET ME KNOW. ⟵ MAYBE THIS SHOWS THAT I DON'T HAVE ENOUGH MOTIVATION.

THANK YOU SO MUCH FOR READING THIS WHOLE THING. SEE YOU IN BOOK 12. ♥

SPECIAL THANKS

HANA-CHAN
YOSHII
KIMURA-SAN
NAKAZAWA-SAN
HITOSHI HAYAKAWA
(BROTHER)

MINE-SAMA
INO-SAMA
SHIOZAWA-SAMA

EVERYBODY FROM THE EDITING DEPARTMENT
EVERYBODY WHO SENT ME LETTERS
EVERYBODY WHO'S READING THIS RIGHT NOW

About the Creator

Tomoko Hayakawa was born on March 4.

Since her debut as a manga creator, Tomoko Hayakawa has worked on many shojo titles with the theme of romantic love—only to realize that she could write about other subjects as well. She decided to pack her newest story with the things she likes most, which led to her current, enormously popular series, *The Wallflower*.

Her favorite things are: Tim Burton's *The Nightmare Before Christmas*, Jean-Paul Gaultier, and samurai dramas on TV. Her hobbies are collecting items with skull designs and watching *bishonen* (beautiful boys). Her dream is to build a mansion like the one the Addams family lives in. Her favorite pastime is to lie around at home with her cat, Ten (whose full name is Tennosuke).

Her zodiac sign is Pisces, and her blood group is AB.

Translation Notes

Japanese is a tricky language for most Westerners, and translation is often more an art than science. For your edification and reading pleasure, here are notes on some of the places where we could have gone in a different direction in our translation of the work, or where a Japanese cultural reference is used.

Sangetan soup, page 38
Sangetan soup is a Korean soup made with chicken, rice, ginseng, nutmeg, and garlic. It's reputed to have energy-rejuvenating properties.

Cho-san, page 50
The author is probably referring to the famous comedian Chousuke Ikariya, who died in 2004, around the time this story first appeared in Japan. The guys are supposed to be watching Cho-san do one of his famous bits on TV.

Hiroshi-kun gets some sun, page 54

In Japan, on sunny days, people hang their futons and comforters outside. It's supposed to dry out the futon and kill any dust mites that might be inhabiting it. Here, the guys are suggesting that Sunako is hanging Hiroshi out to dry just as she would a futon.

Can of coffee and peanut and cracker snacks, page 54

Canned coffee beverages are extraordinarily popular in Japan, and there are numerous brands. Many American stars have done Japanese canned coffee commercials. The "peanut and cracker snacks" Yuki refers to are a delicious snack called *kakipii,* a mix of peanuts and tiny rice crackers.

Hachiouji, page 61

Hachiouji is a suburb on the outskirts of Tokyo.

Instant rice porridge, page 62

Rice porridge, called *okayu* in Japanese, is commonly fed to sick people. It's sort of a Japanese version of chicken soup.

Addressing envelopes, page 129

Sunako got a job addressing envelopes. This used to be a common "work from home" job in Japan.

Movie theater programs, page 145

Japanese movie theaters often sell programs for each movie they feature. The programs contain background information on the film and photos.

Yakitori, page 147

Sunako and Kyohei are at a *yakitori* restaurant. *Yakitori* literally means "grilled chicken." *Yakitori* restaurants can be found all over Japan.

Batting cage, page 152

Batting centers are a popular form of recreation in Japan.

Preview of volume 12

We're pleased to present you a preview from volume 12. This volume is available in English now!

FREE COLLARS KINGDOM

TAKUYA FUJIMI

THOSE FEISTY FELINES!

It's hard to resist Cyan: He's an adorable catboy, whose cute ears and tail have made him a beloved pet. But then his family abandons him, leaving the innocent Cyan to fend for himself.

Just when Cyan thinks he's all alone in the world, he meets the Free Collars, a cool gang of stray cats who believe that no feline should allow a human to imprison his Wild Spirit. They invite Cyan to join them, and the reluctant housecat has to decide fast, because a rival gang of cats is threatening the Free Collars' territory! Can Cyan learn to free his Wild Spirit—and help his new friends save their home?

Special extras in each volume! Read them all!

TOMARE!

止まれ

[STOP!]

You're going the wrong way!

Manga is a completely different
type of reading experience.

To start at the beginning,
go to the end!

That's right! Authentic manga is read the traditional Japanese way—
from right to left. Exactly the opposite of how American books are
read. It's easy to follow: Just go to the other end of the book, and read
each page—and each panel—from right side to left side, starting at
the top right. Now you're experiencing manga as it was meant to be!